CABOOSE DATA BOOK NO. 1

CABOOSES OF THE NEW HAVEN
and
NEW YORK CENTRAL RAILROADS

Published By N.J. INTERNATIONAL, INC.

*#3016/*Collection of H.F. Cavenaugh

IBSN 0-934088-04-7

Cover photo by: H.F. Cavenaugh

Published by N.J. INTERNATIONAL
22 West Nicholai St., Hicksville, N.Y. 10004
Art production and layout by Leeward Enterprises.

All photos credited to PENNSYLVANIA photos may be obtained from Pennsylvania Photos, P.O. Box 823, New York, NY 10004.

CABOOSES OF THE

NEW HAVEN Wood Caboose—Class NE

C-224/Collection of Lew Walter

C-118 (*March 1958*)/Collection of Pete McLachlan

NEW HAVEN Wood Caboose—Class NE

C-1 to C-269

Scale: 3.5mm (1:87) full size for **HO gauge**

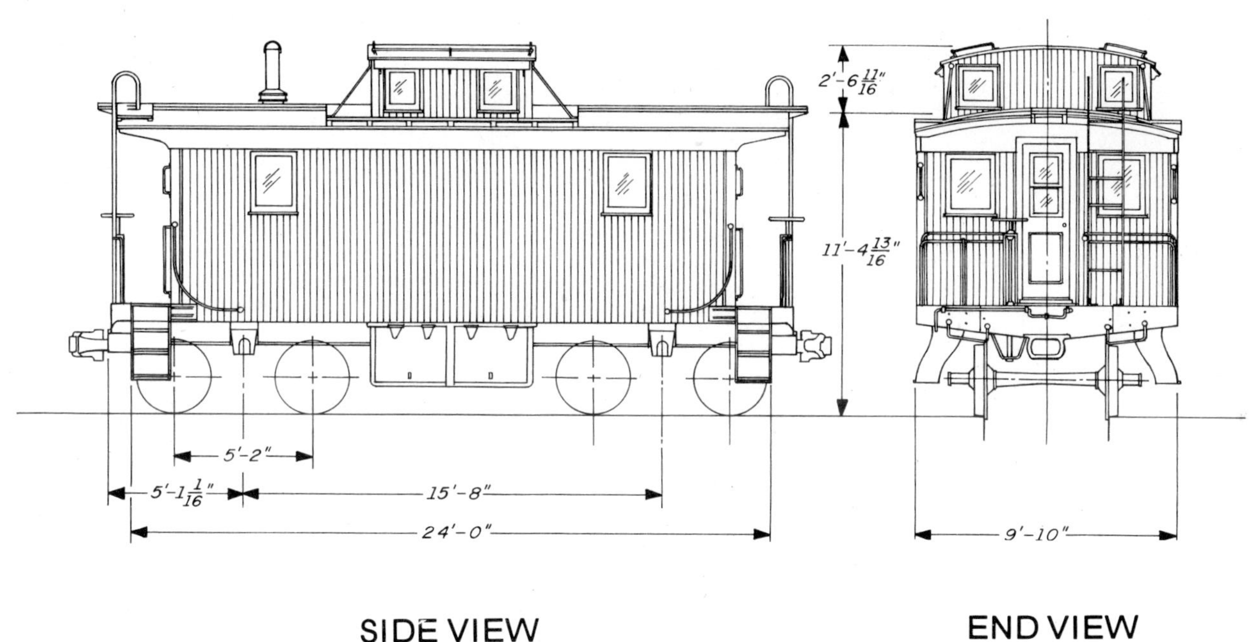

- Built by the New Haven Railroad at their Readville Shops 1922
- Original road numbers 500249 to 500600
- Trucks—Arch Bar type also cast steel type
- Air Brakes—Westinghouse, 8'' X 12'' cylinder

NEW HAVEN Wood Caboose—Class NE

C-149 (9 July, 1933)/Collection of George E. Votava

NEW HAVEN Steel Caboose—Class NE-2

C-500 (March, 1958) / Collection of Pete McLachlan

NEW HAVEN Steel Caboose—Class NE-2

*C-500/*Collection of Pennsylvania Photos

NEW HAVEN Steel Caboose—Class NE-2

C-500 to C-505

Scale: 3.5mm (1:87) full size for HO gauge

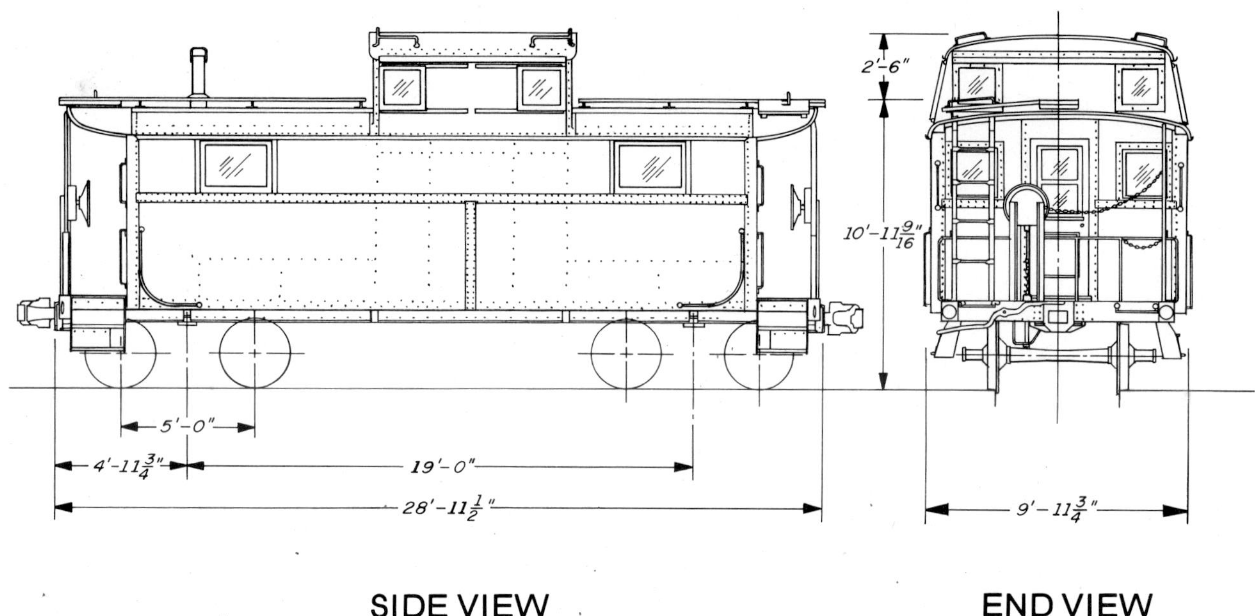

- Built by Keith Car & Mfg Co. 1923
- Trucks—cast steel equalized with swing bolster
- Air Brakes—Westinghouse KD type 10'' X 12'' cylinder
- Hand brake Ajax

NEW HAVEN Steel Caboose—Class NE-3

W-317 (25 March, 1978)/Collection of John Scala

NEW HAVEN Steel Caboose—Class NE-3
C-506 to C-509

Scale: 3.5mm (1:87) full size for **HO** gauge

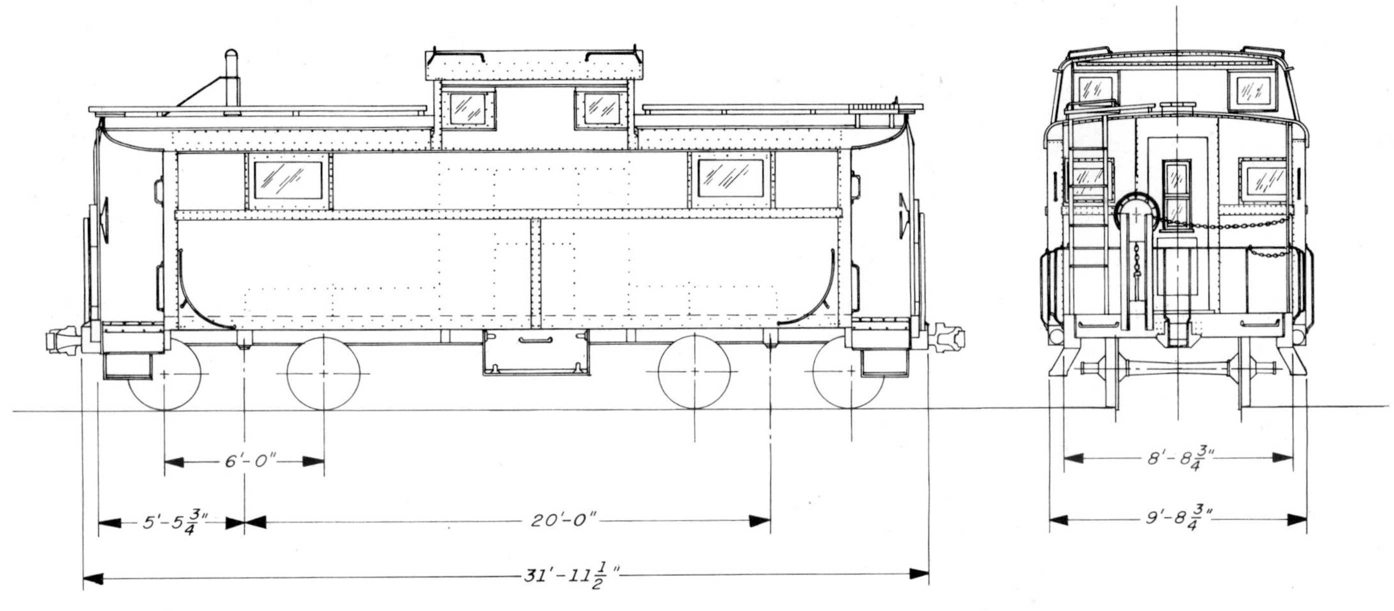

- Built by Osgood—Branlet 1928
- Trucks—cast steel—Swing Bolster
- Air Brakes—Westinghouse, KD type 10'' X 12'' cylinder
- Hand brake—Ajax

NEW HAVEN Steel Caboose—Class NE-3

Ex-New Haven W-317 Cedar Hill Yards, New Haven, Conn. (June 1978)/
John Scala

NEW HAVEN Wood Caboose—Class NE-4

C-356 (24 May, 1933)/George E. Votava

NEW HAVEN Wood Caboose—Class NE-4

C-386/Collection of Lew Walter

NEW HAVEN Wood Caboose—Class NE-4

C-300 to C-419

Scale: 3.5mm (1:87) full size for HO gauge

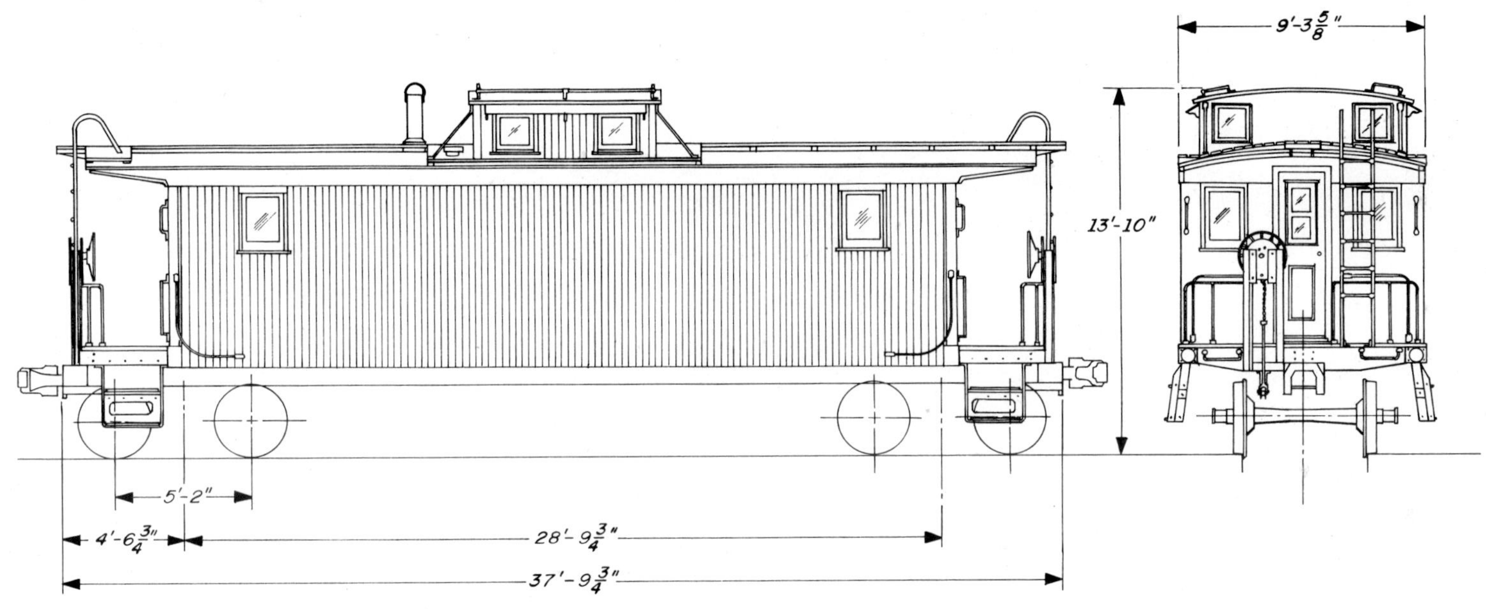

- Built by the New Haven Railroad at their East Hartford Shops 1926-1928
- Steel underframe for old wood box cars
- Original road numbers 501001 to 501120
- Trucks—Arch Bar
- Air Brakes—Westinghouse, KD type 8'' X 12'' cylinder

NEW HAVEN Steel Caboose—Class NE-5

C-583/Collection of H.F. Cavenaugh

C-517/Collection of H.F. Cavenaugh

NEW HAVEN Steel Caboose—Class NE-5

C-510 to C-634

Scale: 3.5mm (1:87) full size for HO gauge

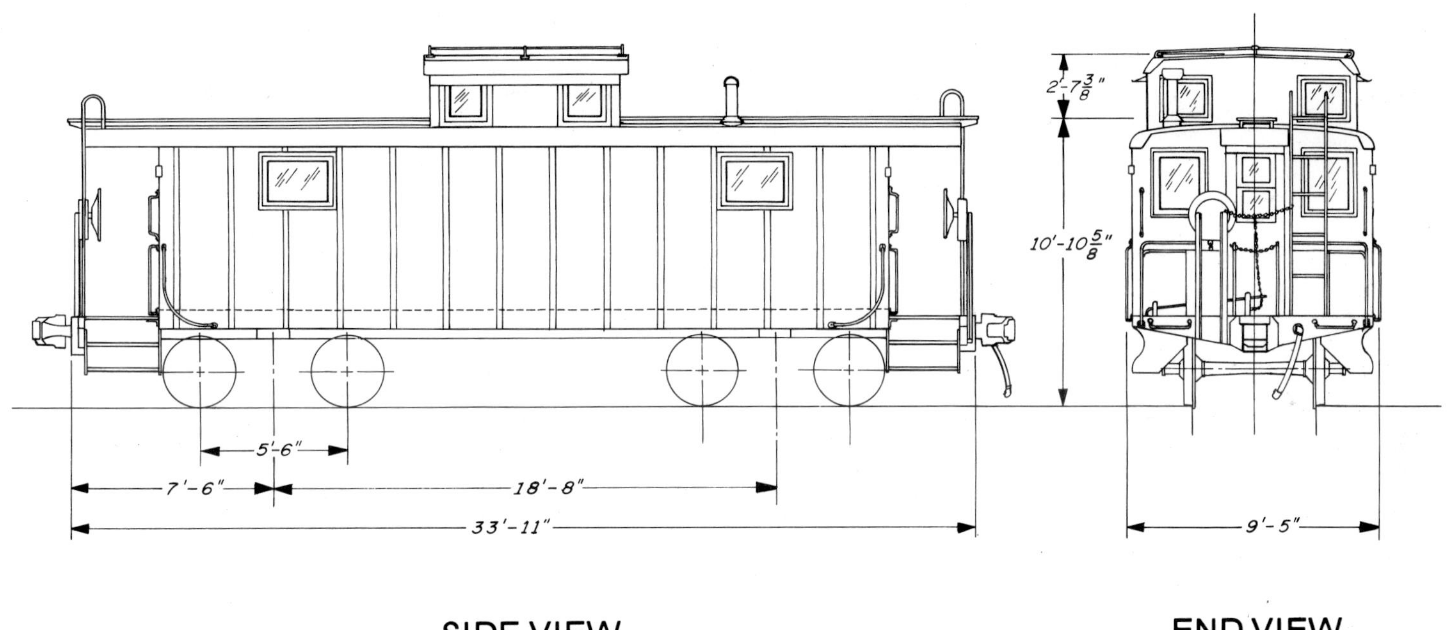

- Built by Pullman Standard Mfg., Co., 1944
- Trucks—Swingmotion type
- Air Brakes—Westinghouse AB type, 10'' X 12'' cylinder
- Hand brake—Ajax type

NEW HAVEN Steel Caboose—Class NE-5

C-528/Collection of John Scala

NEW HAVEN Steel Caboose—Class NE-6

C-665/Collection of Pennsylvania Photos

NEW HAVEN Steel Caboose—Class NE-6

NH3-68/ Collection of H.F. Cavenaugh

*C-664/*Collection of Pennsylvania photos

*C-637/*Collection of Pennsylvania photos

NEW HAVEN Steel Caboose—Class NE-6
C-635 to C-709

Scale: 3.5mm (1:87) full size for HO gauge

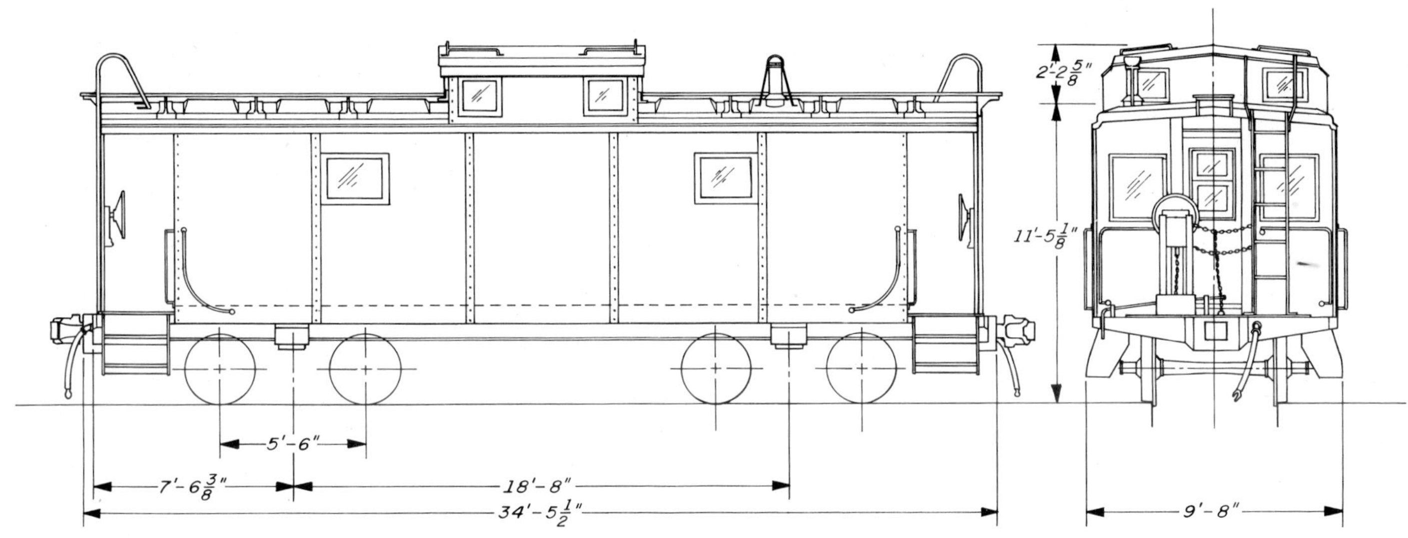

SIDE VIEW

END VIEW

- Built by International Car & Equip., Co., 1947-1948
- Trucks—Swingmotion type
- Air Brakes—Westinghouse AB type 10'' X 12'' cylinder
- Hand brake—Ajax

NEW HAVEN Steel Caboose—Class NE-6

NH1-43/Collection of H.F. Cavenaugh

CABOOSES OF THE

NEW YORK CENTRAL Standard Wood Caboose

*NYC #3-25/*Collection of H.F. Cavenaugh

NEW YORK CENTRAL Standard Wood Caboose
19000 Series

Scale: 3.5mm (1:87) full size for HO gauge

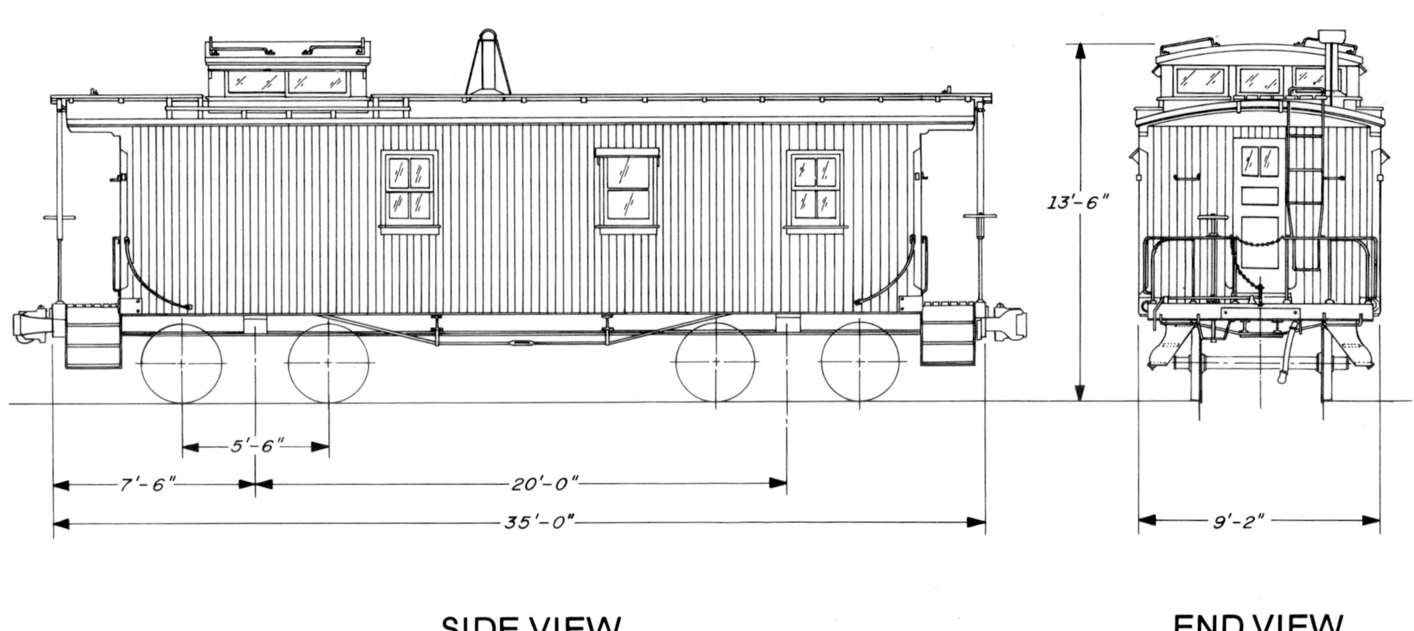

SIDE VIEW   END VIEW

- Built 1872-1925, last several hand built at Oswego
- Trucks—"T" Section NYC Caboose Trucks
- Air Brakes—Westinghouse, KC type

NEW YORK CENTRAL Standard Wood Caboose

#17042/Collection of George E. Votava

Interior showing pot bellied stove, fire wood chest and trainman's desk./Collection of H.F. Cavenaugh

#19400/Collection of H.F. Cavenaugh

NEW YORK CENTRAL Standard Wood Caboose

*#21 (Feb. 1959)/*Collection of H.F. Cavenaugh

NEW YORK CENTRAL Short Standard Wood Caboose

#18314/Collection of Paul W. Prescott

#18168/Collection of Paul W. Prescott

NEW YORK CENTRAL Short Standard Wood Caboose
18000 Series

Scale: 3.5mm (1:87) full size for HO gauge

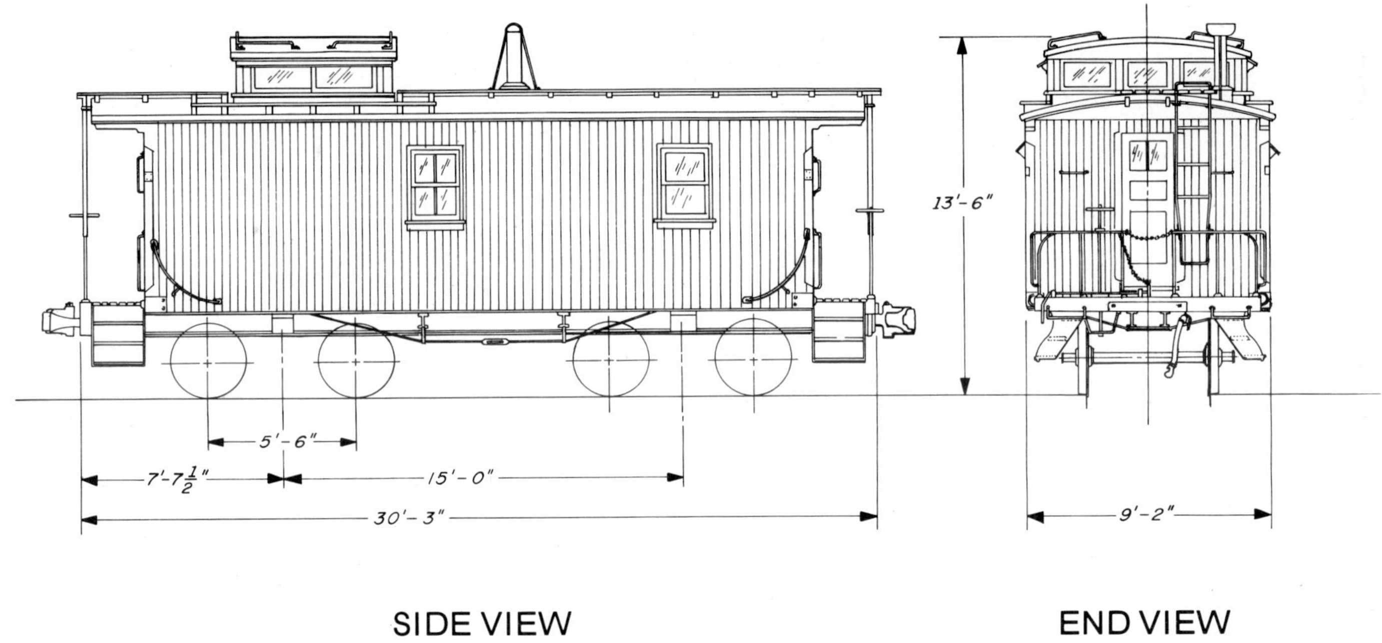

- Rebuilt from ex LS&MS Cabooses. Originally built Collinwood, Ohio, 1902-1906
- Underbody—Steel frame with truss rods

NEW YORK CENTRAL Converted Wood Caboose

*#20107/*Schreiber negative, in Shade collection.

*#20118/*Collection of Harold K. Vollrath

NEW YORK CENTRAL Converted Wood Caboose
20100 to 20149

Scale: 3.5mm (1:87) full size for HO gauge

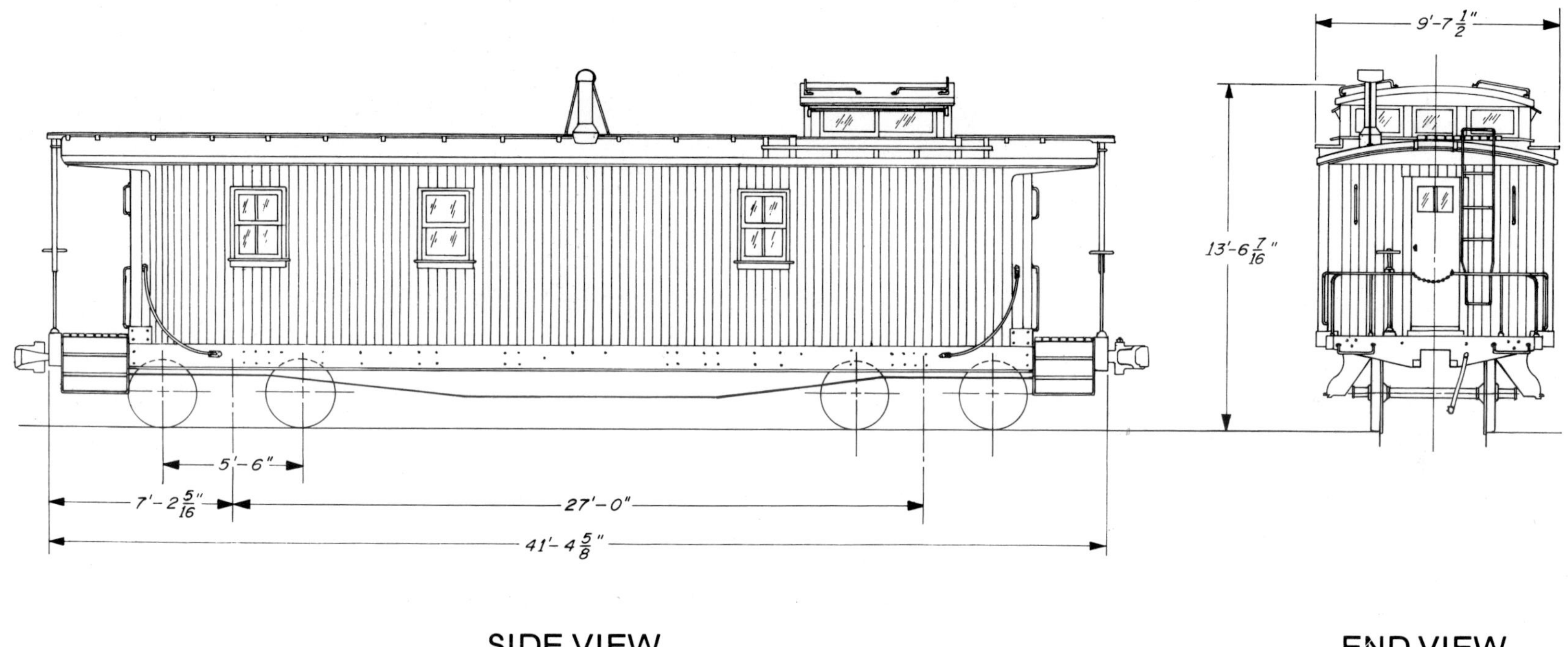

- Built—Rebuilt by NYC from old box cars in their East Buffalo Shops, 1944
- Underbody—steel frame

NEW YORK CENTRAL ''Pacemaker'' Wood Caboose

*#20112/*Collection of Dave Elhardt

NEW YORK CENTRAL ''Pacemaker'' Wood Caboose

*#20133/*Collection of Paul W. Prescott

NEW YORK CENTRAL ''Pacemaker'' Wood Caboose

#20112/Ed Nowak

NEW YORK CENTRAL ''Pacemaker'' Wood Caboose
20112, 20117, 20129, 20132, 20133

Scale: 3.5mm (1:87) full size for HO gauge

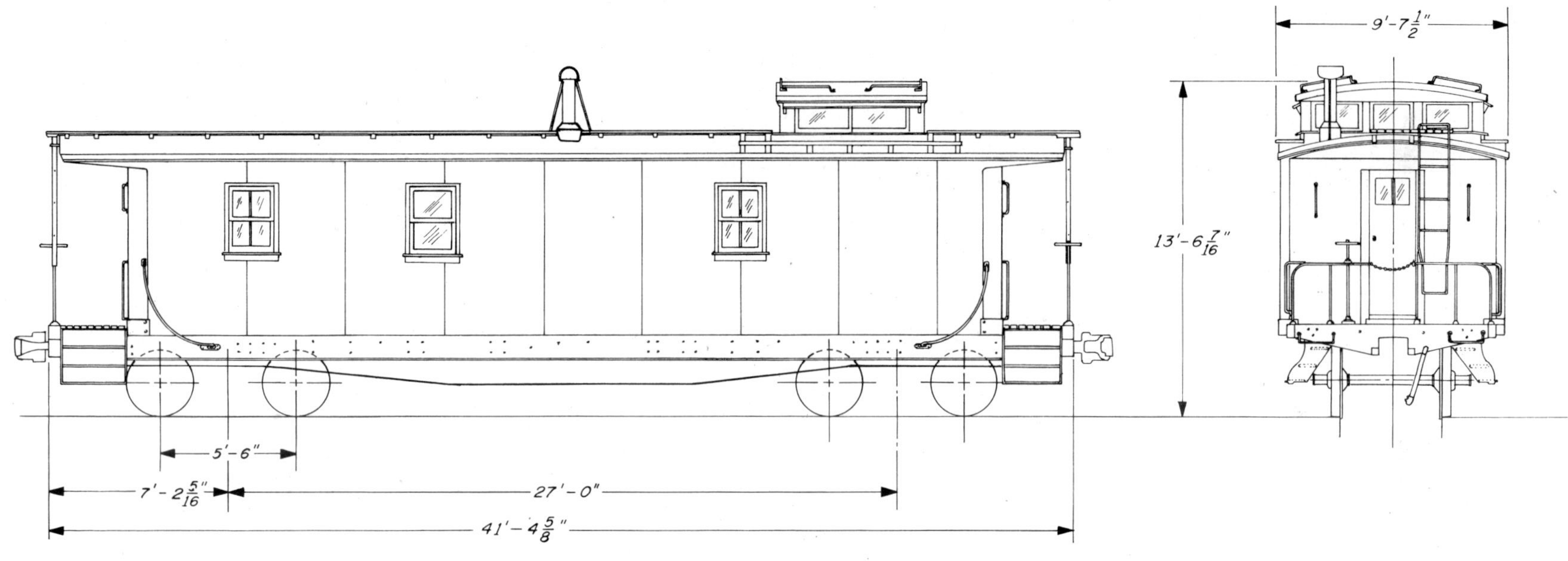

- Converted box cars—plywood sheathing
- Painted vermillion and grey
- Equipped with AB brake system
- Trucks—Barber Bettendorf type

NEW YORK CENTRAL Steel Bay Window Caboose

#20368/Collection of Dave Elhardt

#B&A—44

NEW YORK CENTRAL Steel Bay Window Caboose
NYC Series 20203-20297
B&A Series 1300-1304

Scale: 3.5mm (1:87) full size for HO gauge

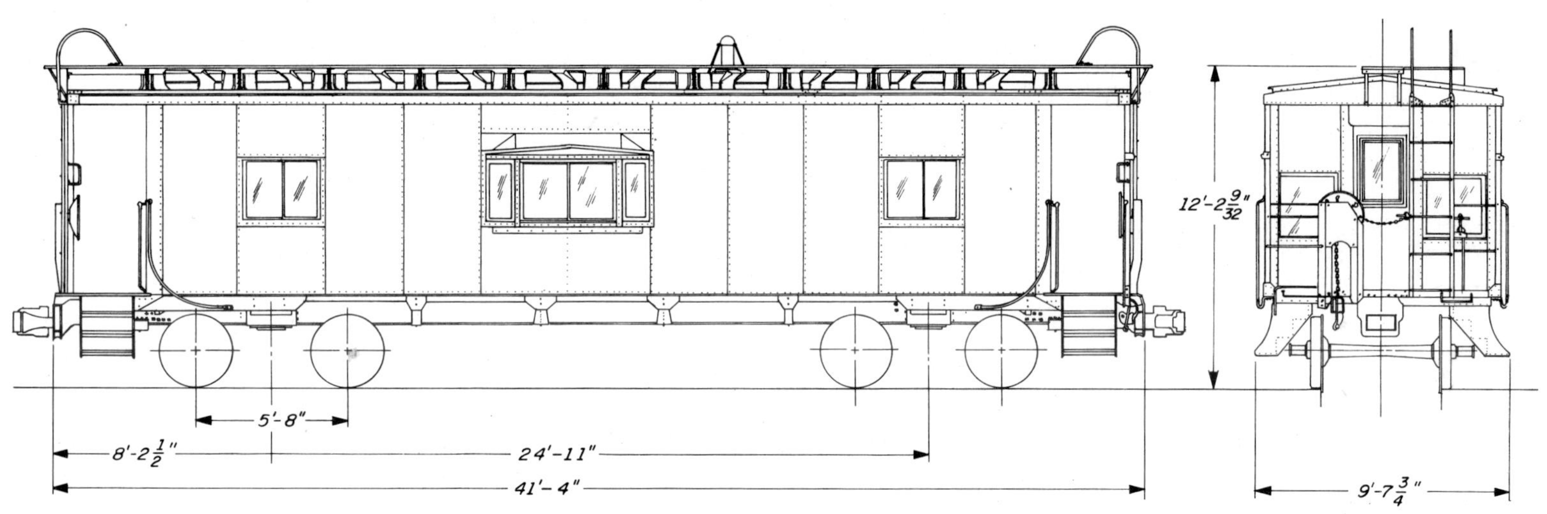

SIDE VIEW   END VIEW

- St. Louis Car Co., 1948-1949
- Trucks—Swingmotion, Barber Bettendorf type
- Equipped with ''AB'' brakes

NEW YORK CENTRAL Steel Bay Window Caboose

#21585/Collection of
Pennsylvania Photos

#21496/Collection of
Pennsylvania Photos

NEW YORK CENTRAL Steel Transfer Caboose

#18098/Collection of Custom Brass

NEW YORK CENTRAL Steel Transfer Caboose

#18072/George E. Votava

#18098/Collection of N/J Custom Brass

#18098/Collection of N/J Custom Brass

NEW YORK CENTRAL Steel Transfer Caboose

Scale: 3.5mm (1:87) full size for HO gauge

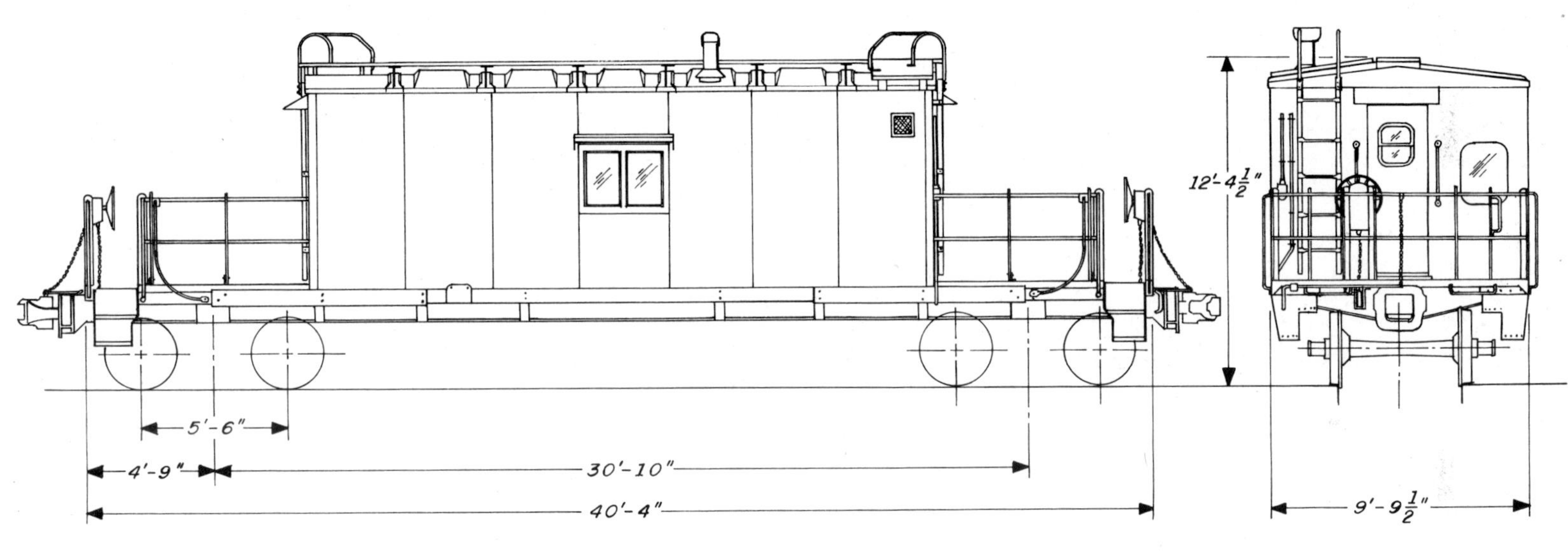

- Built by NYC
- Trucks—Bettendorf freight car trucks
- Equipped with ''AB'' brakes

NEW YORK CENTRAL Steel Transfer Caboose

#18538 (Harmon Yard, Sept. 1974)

AAR STANDARDS
for
CABOOSE BRAKE SYSTEMS
and
SAFETY APPLIANCES

Air Brakes

Caboose air brake systems are made up of various detail parts which make up complete brake systems. These systems are divided into two general groups.
  (1) Pneumatic operating devices, with their associated piping and accessories
  (2) Foundation, brake rigging, levers, rods, brake beams and other parts used to transmit pressure from the brake cylinder piston to the brake shoes.

The necessity for accurate and positive control of rolling stock requires the use of efficient braking systems. Over the years this has led to the development of the modern air brake system. The use of air brakes is compulsory on American railroads.

Air Brake Systems—the term air brakes covers any brake operated by air pressure, but usually is restricted to systems of continuous brakes operated by compressed air (these are distinctly different from vacuum brakes, which are operated by creating a vacuum). Air is compressed by air pumps, single or compound (on steam locomotives) by motor compressor (on electric and diesel locomotives) and, conveyed by pipes and flexible hoses between cars to cylinders and pistons under each car, by which the pressure is transmitted to the brake levers and then to the brake shoes.

Types of Air Brake Systems

Straight Air Brake—this is the original form of Westinghouse air brake. With this system, the compressed air is used as a direct force from the main reservoir supply of the locomotive, through direct piping to the brake cylinders on each car to apply the brakes. The valve in the locomotive is used to admit air to the brake pipes, and brake cylinders in order to apply the brakes, to hold it there when admitted, and to exhaust it when desiring to release the brakes. This form of brake was superseded by the plain automatic air brake, and is rarely used.

Automatic Air Brake—this system is designed so that the brakes will be applied automatically in case air escapes from the system. To accomplish this, an auxiliary reservoir is added to each car, in which is stored a supply of compressed air sufficient to operate the brakes on that car, and a triple valve to which the brake pipe, auxiliary reservoir and brake cylinder are all connected. The brake is applied by reducing pressure in the brake pipe below that in the auxiliary reservoirs, caused by venting to the atmosphere by the engineer or accidently by a broken hose or pipe. The resulting reduction in brake pipe pressure destroys the equilibrium between the brake pipe and auxiliary reservoir pressure. The auxiliary reservoir pressure, now being greater, causes the triple valve in each car to operate, and applies the brakes by admitting air to the brake cylinders.

Quick Action Automatic Air Brake—in this type system the triple valve is modified so that when a relatively quick reduction in brake pipe pressure is made, it also opens a direct communication from the brake pipe through the triple valve to the brake cylinder. This not only increases the brake cylinder pressure in proportion to the amount of air flowing into it from the brake pipe locally on each car, but by venting air from the brake pipe locally on each car, hastens and increases the effect of the reduction made by the brake valve. This shortens the time from the movement of the brake valve handle until a full brake application is obtained on the entire train, and increases the total braking power obtainable by such an operation—emergency application. The present standard freight car brake is the ''AB'' type. This has been required on cars built after September 1, 1933 and in all cars interchanged after January 1, 1945.

Triple Valve—this component is one of the most important parts of the air brake system. It is composed of a body, which has connections to the brake pipe, the auxiliary reservoir and the brake cylinder, in which a slide valve is operated by a piston, so that when pressure in the air brake pipe is increased the auxiliary reservoir is charged and the air in the brake cylinder is released to the atmosphere. When air pressure in the brake pipe is reduced, air from the auxiliary reservoir is discharged into the brake cylinder, applying the brakes. This is called a plain triple valve.

The quick action triple valve has all the above features and performs all the functions of the plain triple valve, but has the additional function of causing a discharge of air from the brake pipe to the brake cylinder, when, the maximum force of the brakes is instantly required, in emergencies. Retarded release and uniform recharge features have been added to the valve.

On modern freight brake equipment, the triple valve has been replaced by the "AB" valve.

Vacuum Brakes—this is a system of continuous brakes operated by exhausting the air from an appliance located under each car, allowing the external air pressure to be transmitted to the brake levers and shoes. An engine mounted ejector is used for exhausting the air in the system. The system maintains a vacuum of 20 to 24 inches of mercury. This type system is obsolete and no longer used on U.S. railroads.

"AB" Brake Systems—in 1926 the American Railway Association (ARA) in cooperation with the Interstate Commerce Commission (ICC), inaugurated a very complete series of tests of various types of air brake equipment for freight train service. The tests were conducted at Purdue University, and were followed by elaborate road tests. The result was the adoption of the "AAR Specifications for Air Brakes" adopted in 1933. The approved freight brake system was designated "AB".

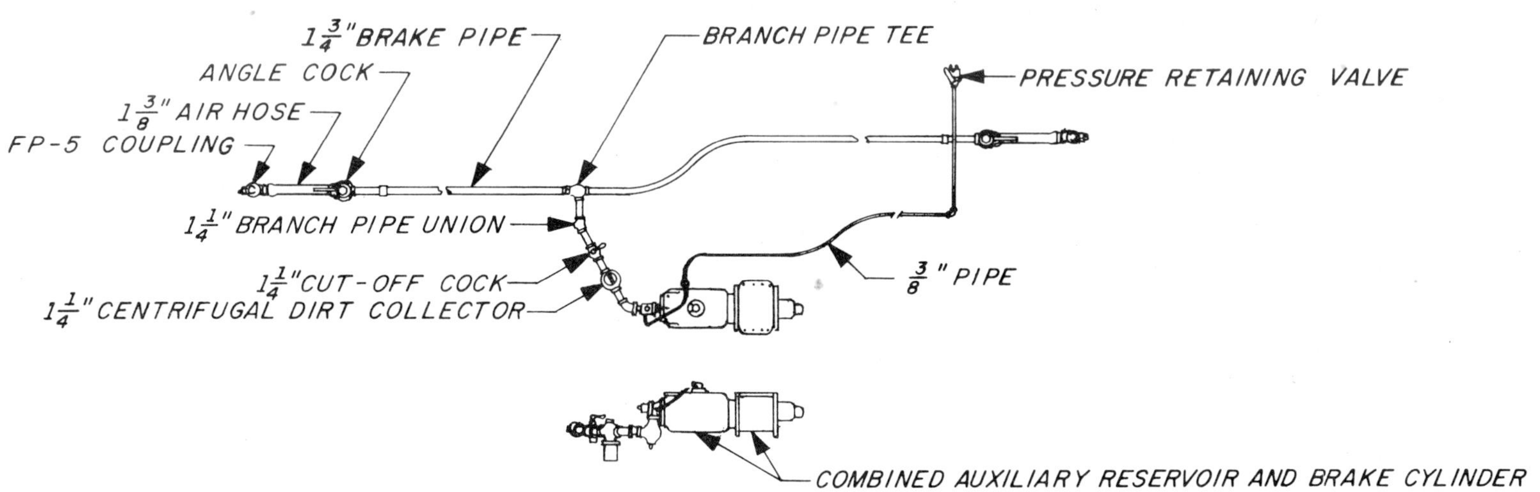

WESTINGHOUSE "KC" AIR BRAKE SYSTEM

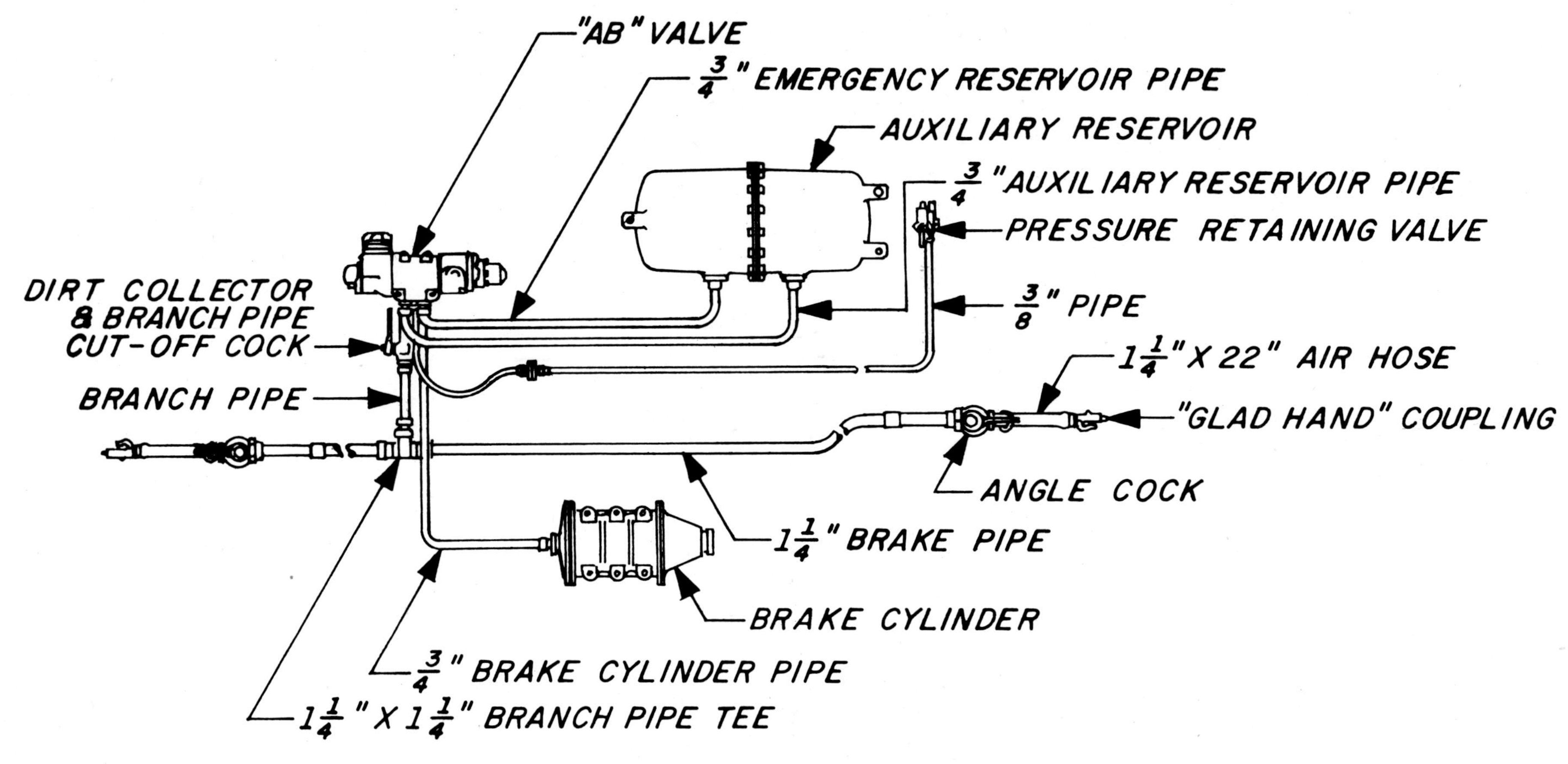

WESTINGHOUSE "AB" AIR BRAKE SYSTEM

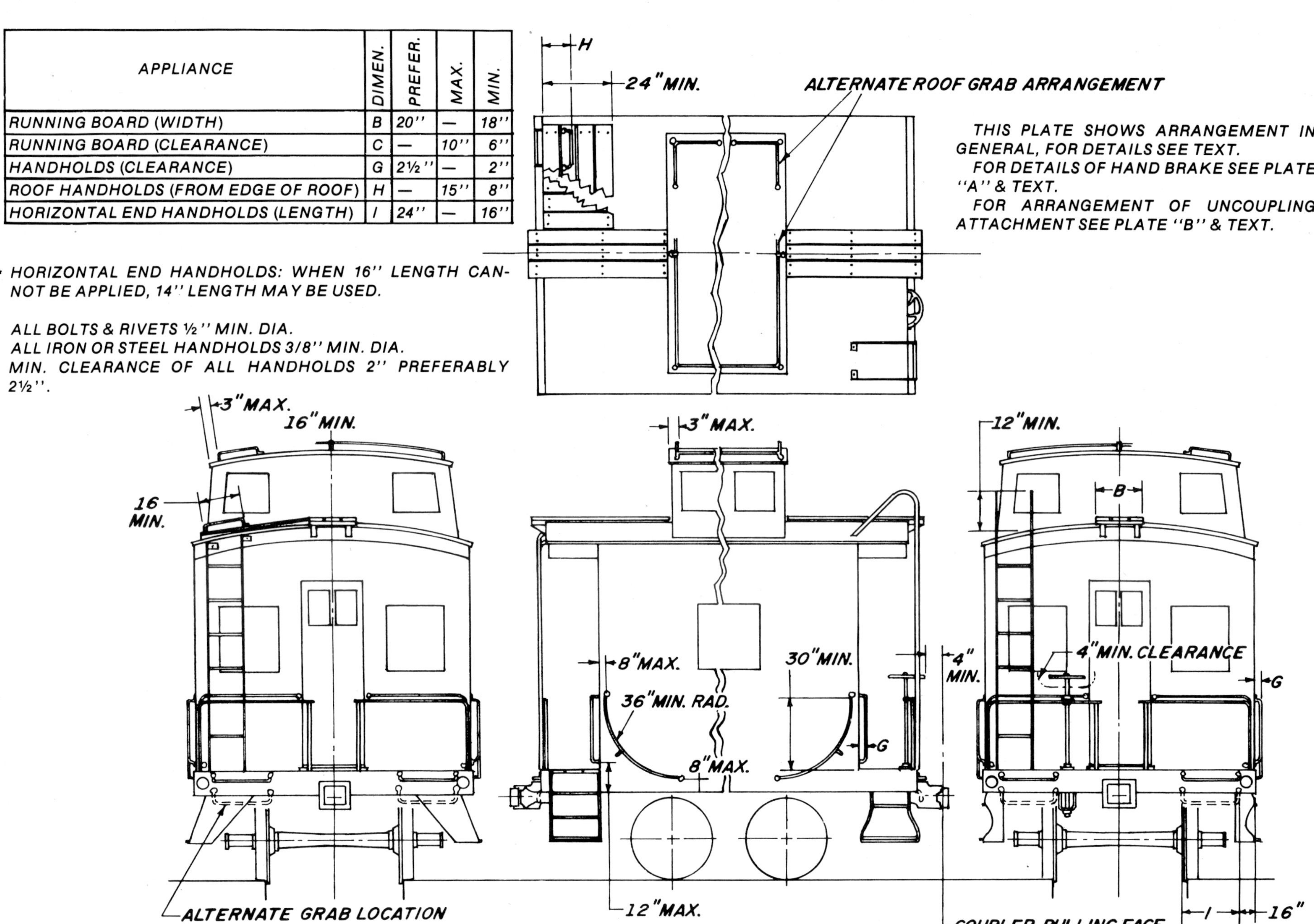

SAFETY APPLIANCES FOR STANDARD CABOOSES

APPLIANCE	DIMEN.	PREFER.	MAX.	MIN.
RUNNING BOARD (WIDTH)	B	20''	—	18''
RUNNING BOARD (CLEARANCE)	C	—	10''	6''
• SILL STEPS (LENGTH OF TREAD)	D	12''	—	10''
SILL STEPS (HEIGHT ABOVE RAIL)	E	22''	24''	—
LADDERS (SPACING FROM ROOF)	F	—	18''	12''
LADDERS & HANDHOLDS (CLEARANCE)	G	2½''	—	2''
ROOF HANDHOLDS (FROM EDGE OF ROOF)	H	—	15''	8''
* HOR. SIDE & END HANDHOLDS (LENGTH)	I	24''	—	16''
HOR. SIDE & END HANDHOLDS (HEIGHT)	J	—	30''	24''

• ADDITIONAL SILL STEP TREAD, WHEN NEEDED, SEE TEXT.
* HORIZONTAL END HANDHOLDS: WHEN 16'' LENGTH CANNOT BE APPLIED, 14'' LENGTH MAY BE USED.

SIDE DOOR STEP BOLTS, ¾'' MIN. DIA.
ALL OTHER BOLTS & RIVETS ½'' MIN. DIA.
BOLTS 3/8'' DIA. MAY BE USED FOR WOODEN TREADS WHICH ARE GAINED INTO STILES.
ALL IRON OR STEEL LADDER TREADS & HANDHOLDS 5/8'' MIN DIA.
MINIMUM CLEARANCE OF ALL LADDER TREADS & HANDHOLDS 2'' PREFERABLY 2½''

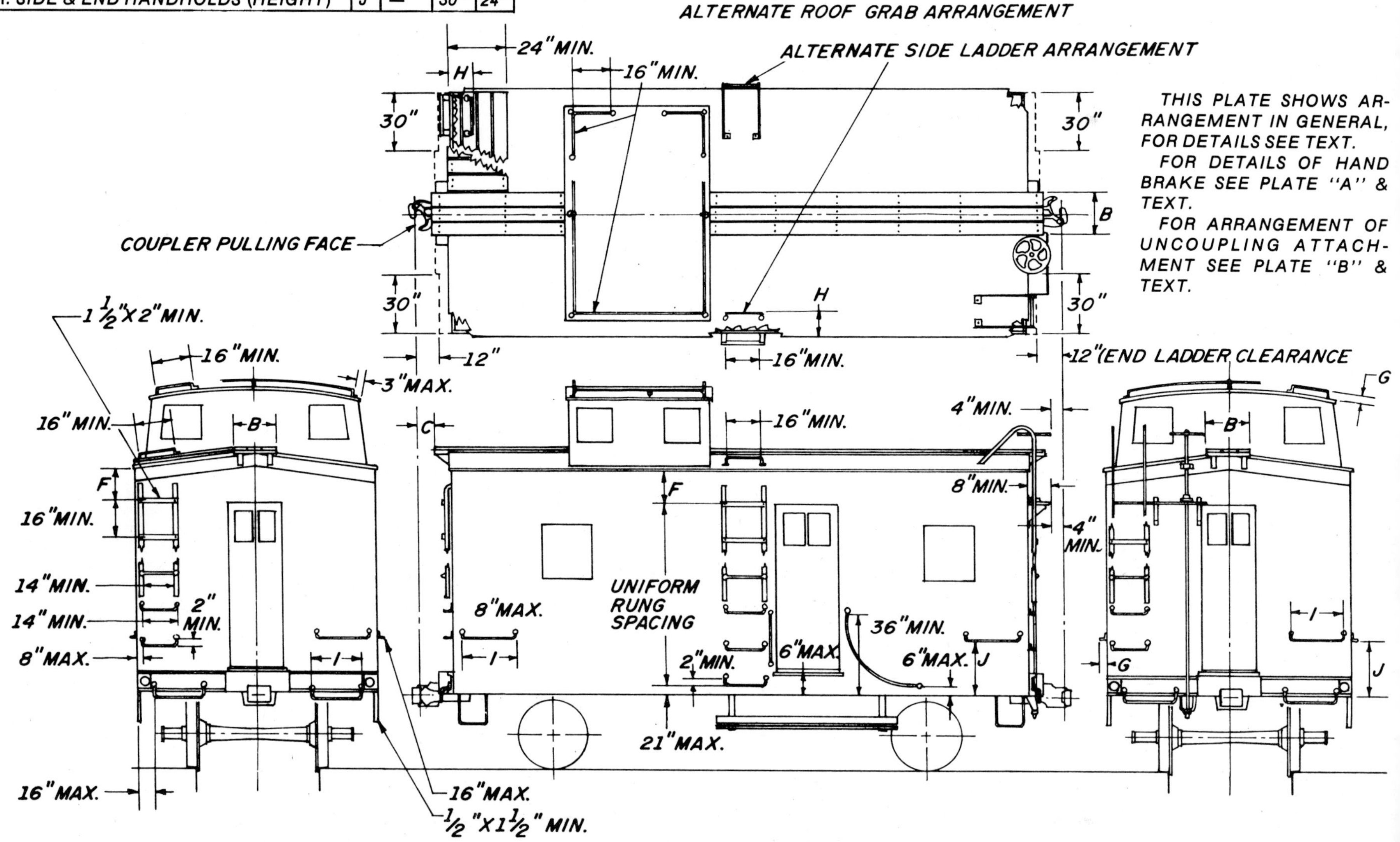

SAFETY APPLIANCES FOR CABOOSES WITHOUT VESTIBULES